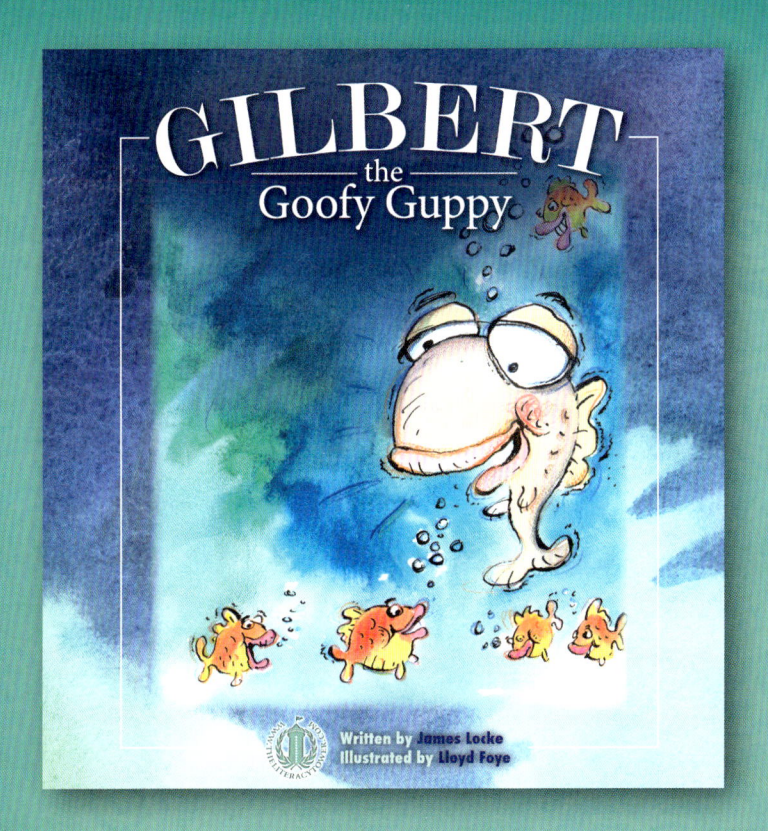

GILBERT
the Goofy Guppy

Written by James Locke
Illustrated by Lloyd Foye

Gilbert

some other fish

something fearsome

"In this book, a fish tells the tale of Gilbert, a goofy guppy. Can you guess what will happen when Gilbert tries to be something he is not?"

Grusilda xxx

Listen carefully as I tell you the tale of Gilbert, a goofy guppy!

One day, Gilbert was not happy. He didn't like being such a small, pale-looking fish.

"No-one takes any notice of me," he gurgled. "Every other fish has bright colours and fancy fins. They don't even want to swim with me."

Gilbert thought hard. Then he had an idea.

"If I was an enormous shark, *every* fish in the sea would take notice of me!"

Gilbert the goofy guppy knew that sharks could swim with their fins sticking out of the water.

Gilbert swam to the top of the sea so *his* fin stuck out of the water.

"Shark, shark, shark!" he yelled. "Look, everyone!"

All the other fish looked at Gilbert. They giggled and grinned and thought Gilbert was goofy.

Gilbert the goofy guppy knew that sharks looked fearsome.

So Gilbert swam to the top of the sea with his fin stuck out of the water *and* he put on his most fearsome face.

"Shark, shark, shark!" he yelled fearsomely.

All the other fish looked at Gilbert. They giggled and grinned and thought Gilbert was even goofier.

Gilbert the goofy guppy knew that sharks had sharp teeth.

So Gilbert swam to the top of the sea with his fin stuck out of the water and he put on his most fearsome face *and* he flashed his sharp teeth.

"Shark, shark, shark!" he yelled fearsomely.

All the other fish looked at Gilbert. They giggled and grinned and still they thought that Gilbert was so goofy.

Gilbert the goofy guppy was determined to try once more. He decided to thrash the water with his tail, just like a shark.

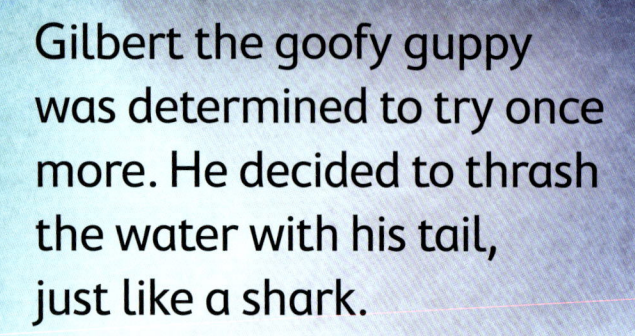

Gilbert swam to the top of the sea, stuck his fin out of the water, put on his most fearsome face, flashed his sharp teeth *and* thrashed the water with his tail.

"Shark, shark, shark!" he yelled furiously.
All the other fish gulped. They gasped. They gurgled.

"Shark, shark, shark!" they all yelled, swimming away as fast as they could.

Gilbert the goofy guppy giggled and grinned.

"At last," he thought. "I finally made those other fish take notice of me. And not only that, they all swam away in fear of little me!"

"Ha!" Gilbert gurgled. "Silly fish. That fooled them."

Gilbert stopped behaving like a big fearsome shark. Suddenly, he felt water surging around him. He swam around to see a …

SHARK, SHARK, SHARK!

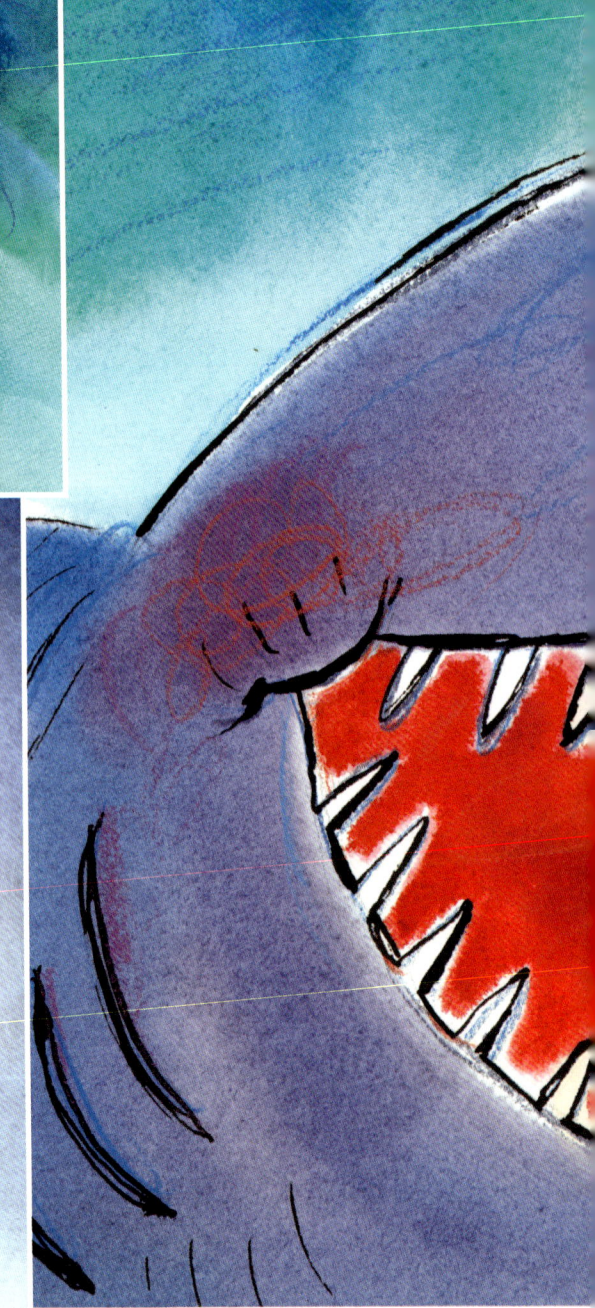

15
fifteen

And that, sadly, is how the tale of Gilbert the goofy guppy ends.

I think Gilbert should have been happy with how he looked, don't you?

By trying to get the attention of all the other small colourful fish, he caught the attention of an even bigger fish – the shark!